MW00885098

THANK YOU FOR CHOOSING US!
WE HOPE YOU ENJOY THIS COLORING BOOK.

THIS BOOK BELONGS TO:

____

____

COLOR TEST PAGE

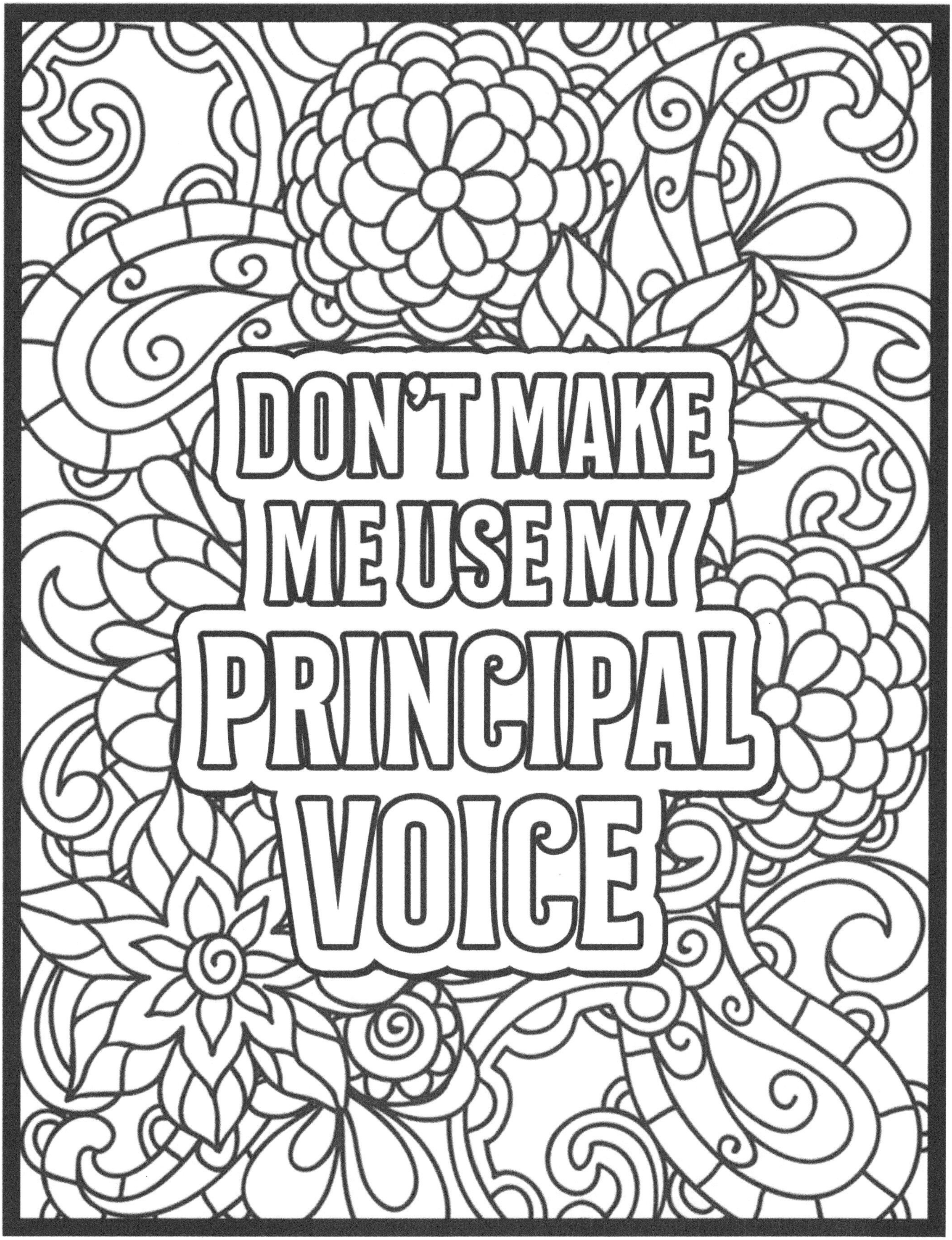
DON'T MAKE
ME USE MY
PRINCIPAL
VOICE

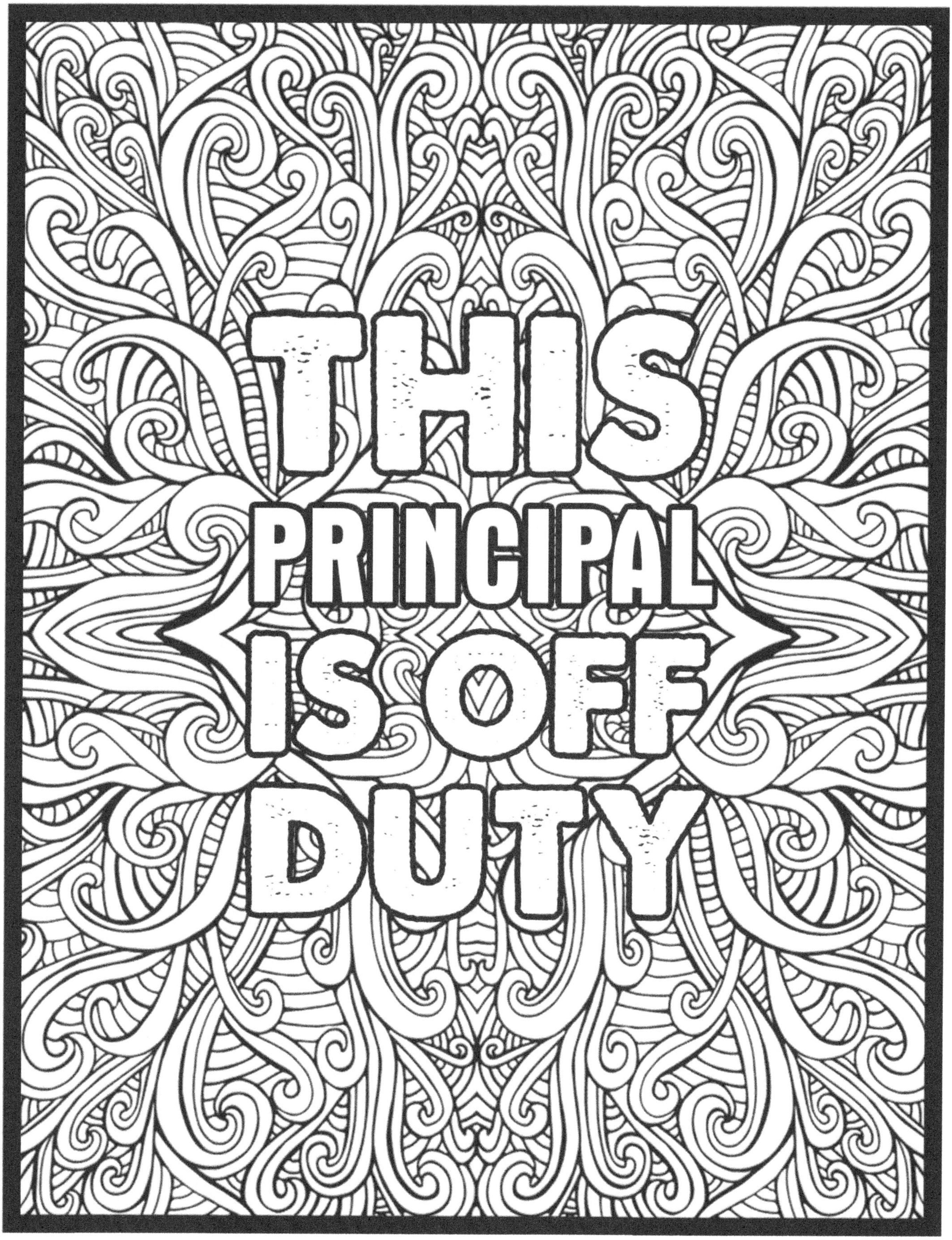
THIS
PRINCIPAL
IS OFF
DUTY

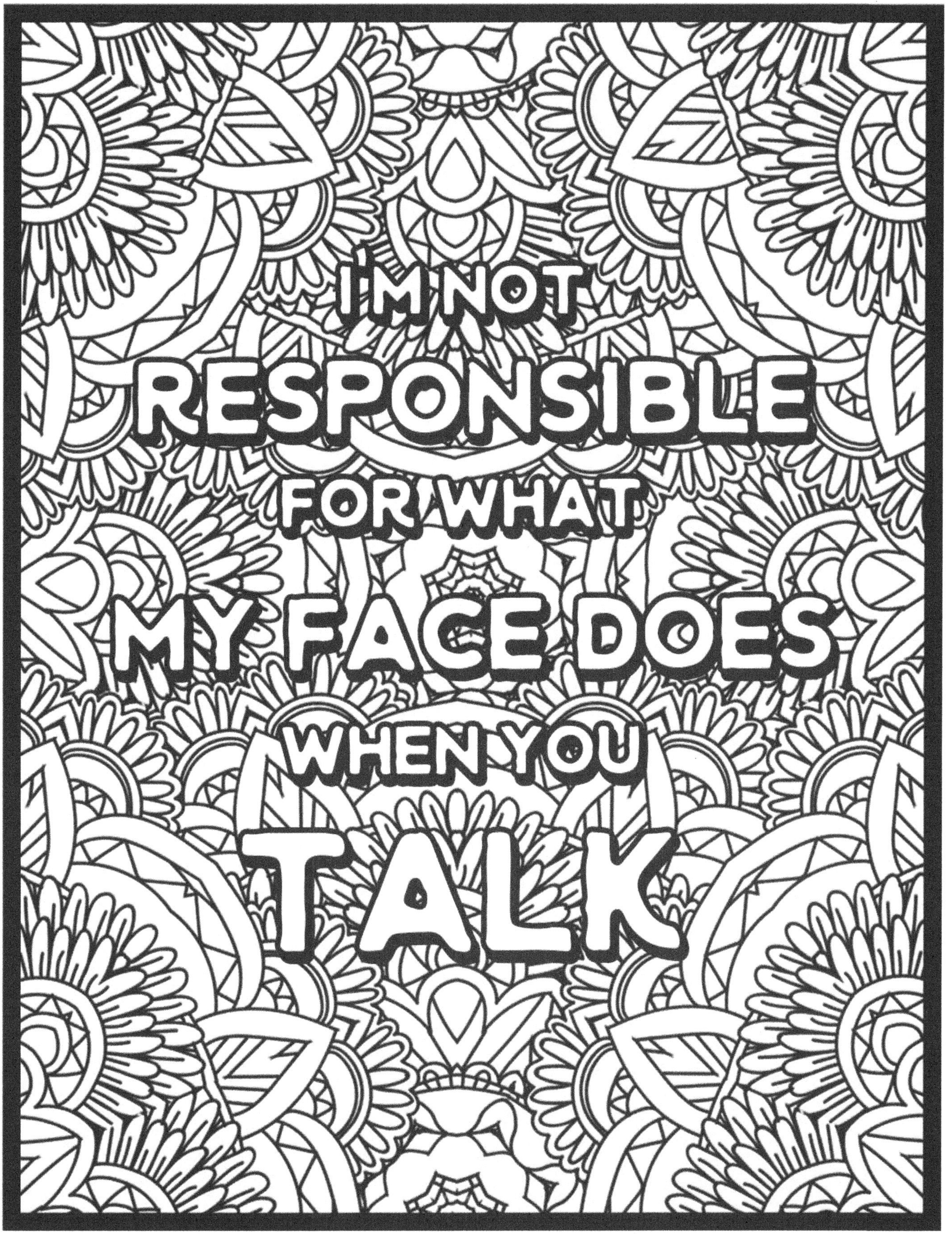
I'M NOT
RESPONSIBLE
FOR WHAT
MY FACE DOES
WHEN YOU
TALK

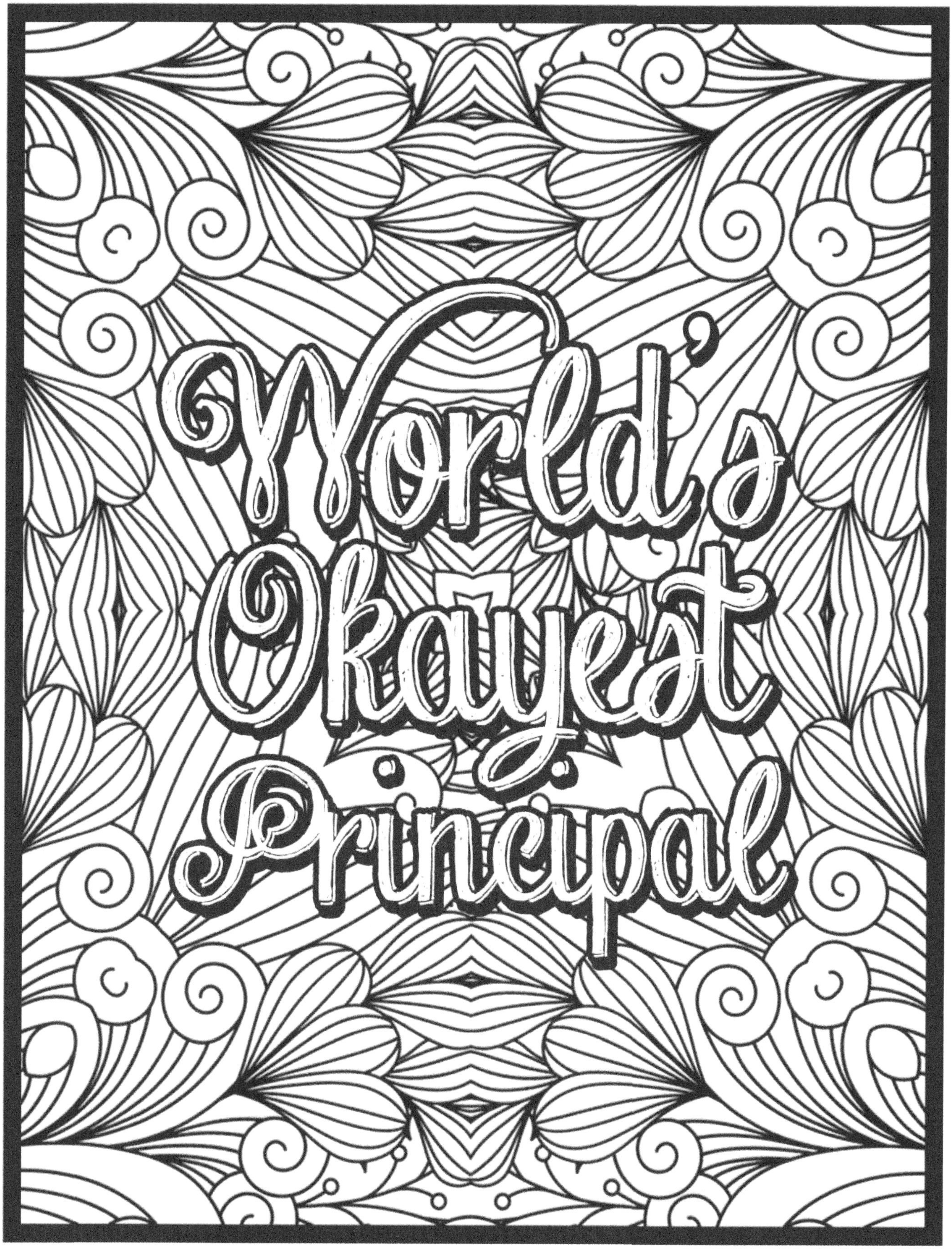
World's
Okayest
Principal

99%
BADASS
01%
PRINCIPAL

MAKE
Today
MAGICAL

SOME PEOPLE
JUST NEED A
HIGH-FIVE
(IN THE FACE)

KEEP
CALM
AND
LEAVE IT
TO THE
PRINCIPAL

FRIDAY.
MY 2ND
FAVORITE
F WORD.

SORRY
I'M DONE
HELPING
ASSHOLES
TODAY

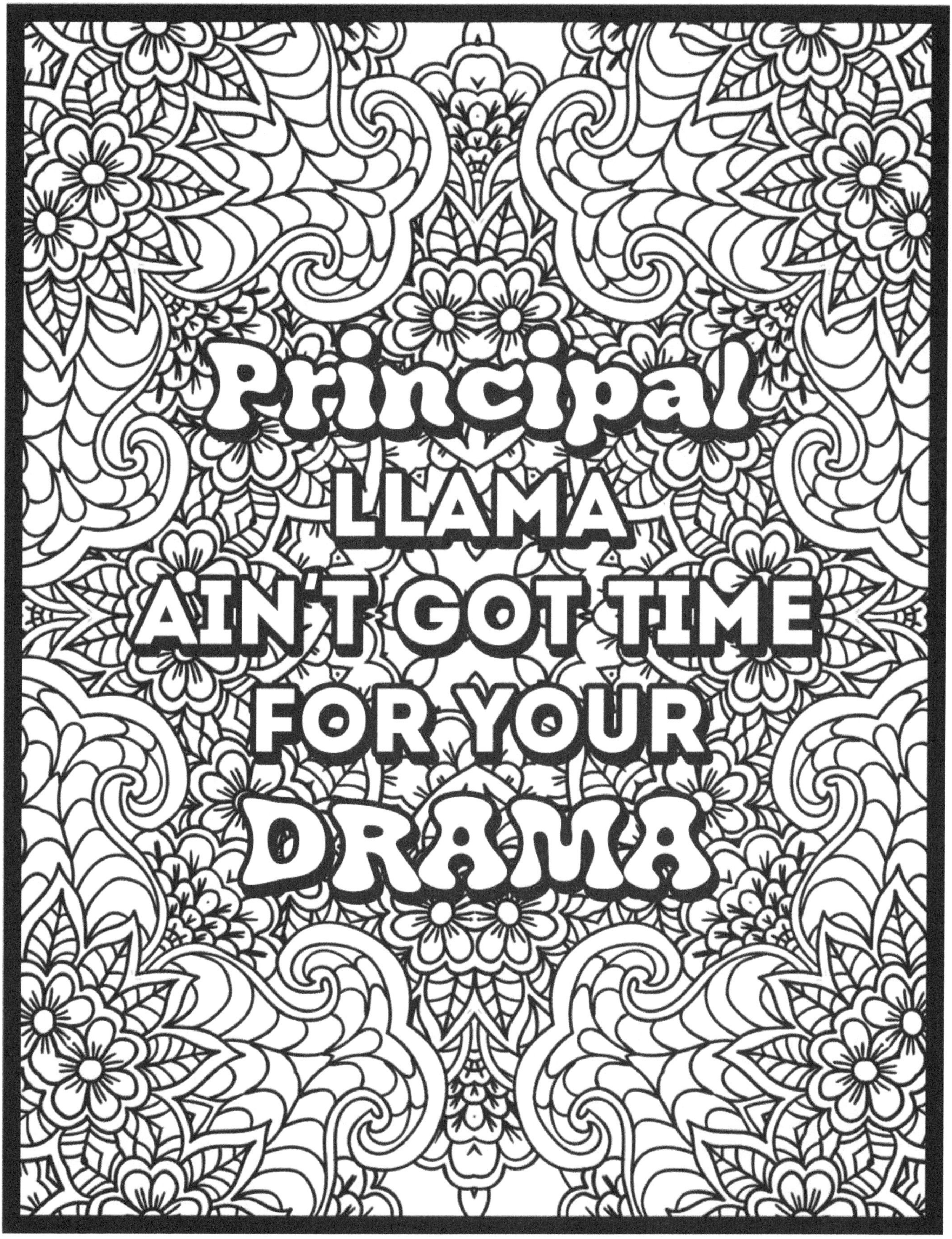
Principal
LLAMA
AIN'T GOT TIME
FOR YOUR
DRAMA

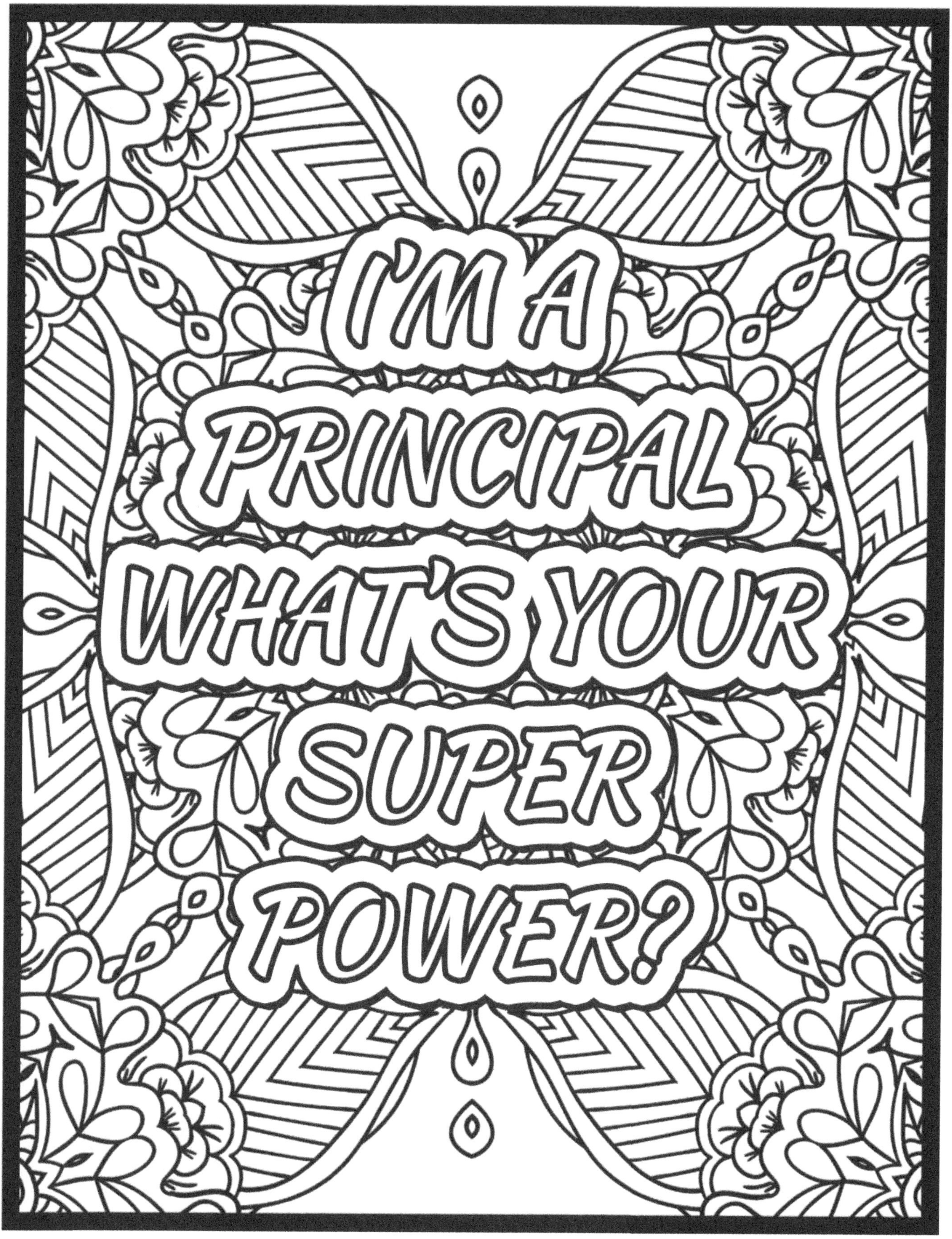
I'M A
PRINCIPAL
WHAT'S YOUR
SUPER
POWER?

Essential
AF

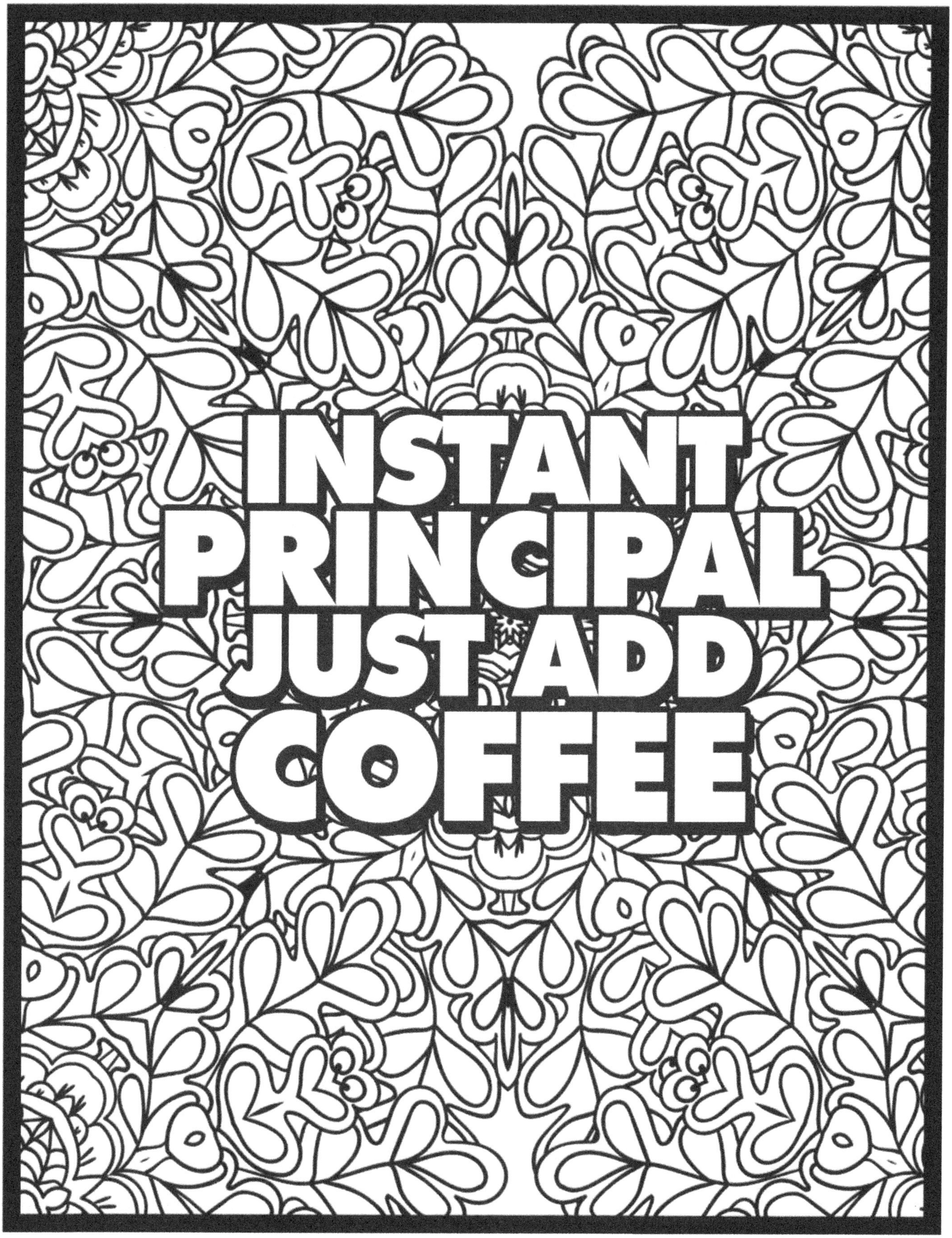
INSTANT
PRINCIPAL
JUST ADD
COFFEE

Work?!
I only
need my
Paychecks.

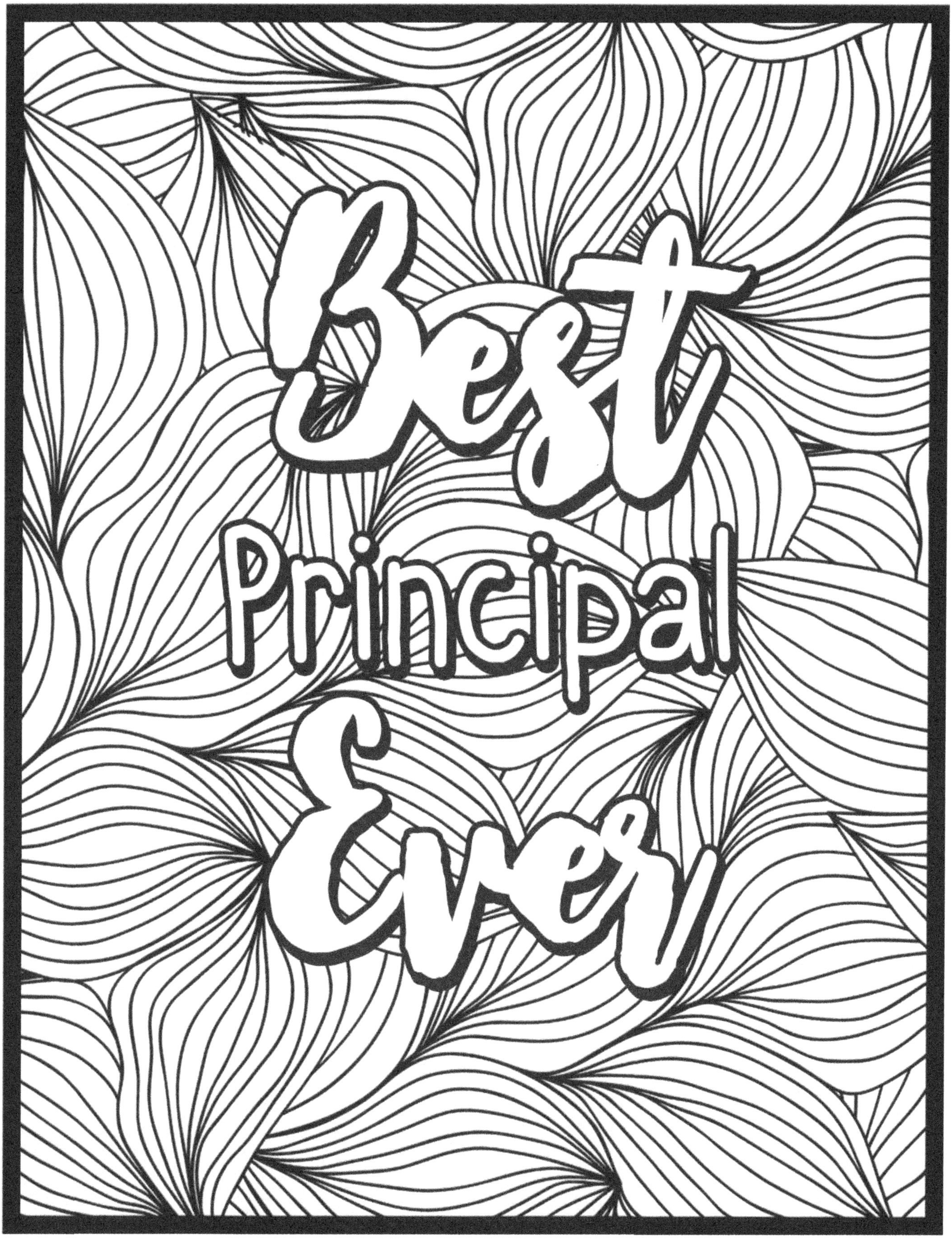
Best
Principal
Ever

I'VE 101
PROBLEMS
BUT
COLORING
AIN'T ONE

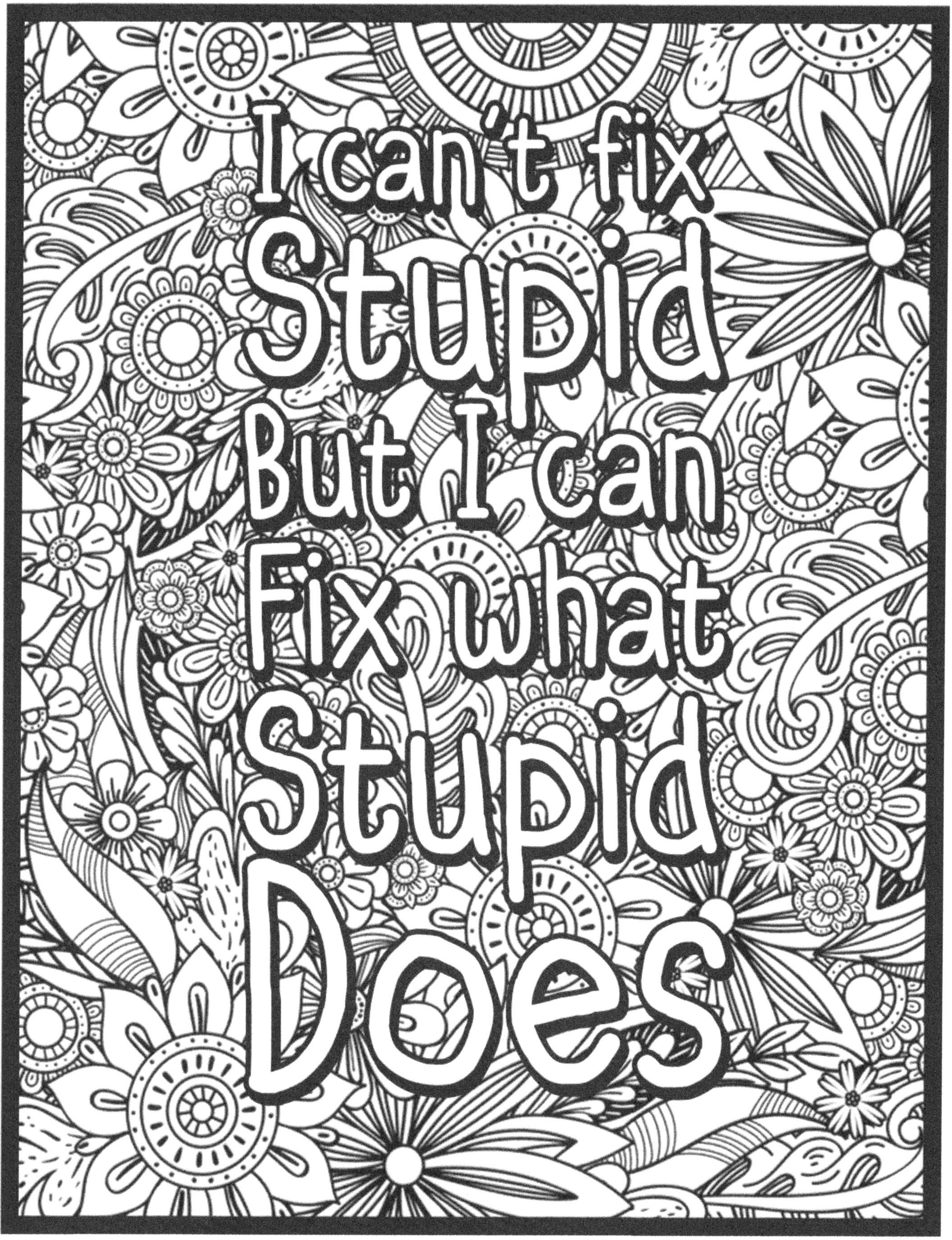
I can't fix
Stupid
But I can
Fix what
Stupid
Does

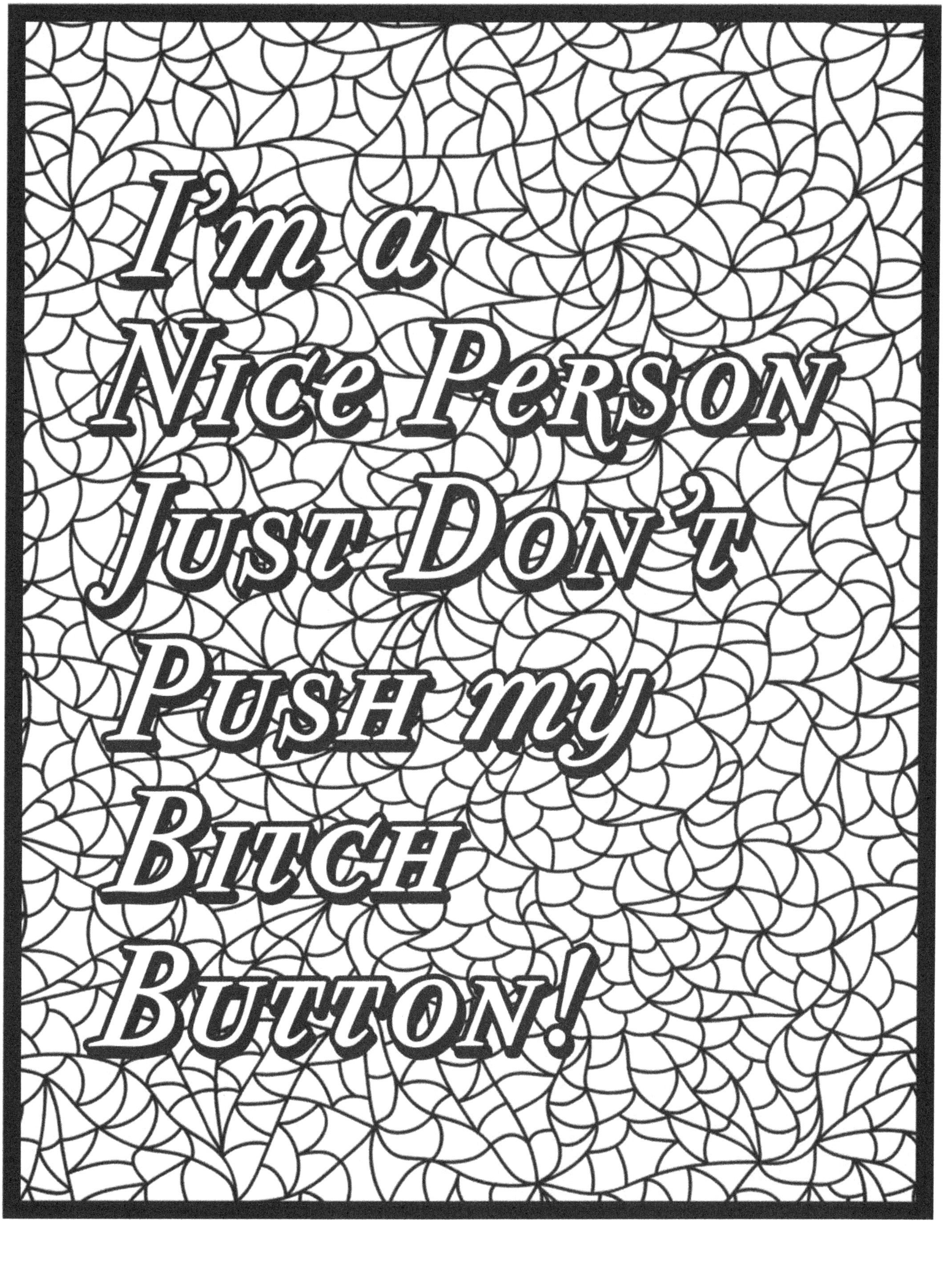
I'm a
Nice Person
Just Don't
Push my
Bitch
Button!

It's a
Principal
Thing
You'd not
Understand

Made in United States
Orlando, FL
29 August 2024

50900097R00026